A Fresh Approach
to Sight-Singing

Joining the Dots
Singing

Grade 1

Alan Bullard

ABRSM

To the Teacher

Joining the Dots Singing offers a wealth of material to help build skill and confidence in sight-singing. Used as part of regular lessons and practice, it will help pupils learn to read new music more quickly and easily, and develop their awareness of rhythm, pitch and other general musicianship skills.

This book is designed to prepare pupils for the sight-singing section of the ABRSM Grade 1 Singing exam, but it will also help instrumentalists to develop their sight-singing skills. While every teacher will have their own approach, pupils who tackle the material in order will – with your help and with regular practice – acquire a sound sight-singing technique.

Each book in the series contains the following mix of technical and creative activities and songs to sing:

Workouts build, step by step, the rhythm and pitch skills required for the grade, and are taught both aurally and from the page. This book focuses on stepwise movement above and below the key-note. The focus of each Workout is identified in a header and then introduced in a 'singing back' exercise for teacher and pupil (if necessary, you could improvise more). A number of short exercises promote effective reading of staff notation using tonic sol-fa, numbered degrees of the scale or any suitable syllable.

Make Music provides an opportunity for pupils to build performing confidence in and through creative and imaginative work. Using an approach that is not primarily notation-based, the activities here will help to familiarize pupils with the 'feel' of a key-centre and the way that pitches relate to it, and to develop their sense of rhythm. You and your pupils can approach these exercises together in whatever way you find most comfortable, perhaps with some trial and error – experimenting is a good way to learn here!

It Takes Two enables two pupils (or pupil and teacher) to work together on the techniques learnt, and to build confidence in singing an independent part using rounds. It also offers the opportunity to practise singing with a piano accompaniment. Your pupils should take as long as necessary preparing the pieces as outlined. Plenty of time taken here, together with lots of practice, will help them to focus on the salient points in an exam sight-singing test, with its shorter preparation time.

Read and Sing provides an invaluable source of sight-singing material for those preparing for the Grade 1 Singing exam. The songs are intended to be sung at sight or after a short practice time, with the focus on keeping going. Each one has a title (unlike those in the exam), and they sometimes have a slightly wider range of colour and detail in the accompaniment, to help pupils reflect the musical mood suggested by the title. To replicate an exam scenario, encourage your pupils to set a tempo they can maintain and follow this in the accompaniment, helping to keep the song going. Some of the Read and Sing material is also provided in the bass clef, for those who wish to develop fluency in reading both clefs. (All the treble-clef material may also be sung an octave lower.)

Songs with Words, the final page, consists of two short songs to learn. The first is a round – enabling several pupils to sing independently – and the second is a song with piano accompaniment. As these are designed to be learnt, they push the boundaries slightly while employing largely the same rhythms and intervals as the material in the rest of the book.

First published in 2015 by ABRSM (Publishing) Ltd, a wholly owned subsidiary of ABRSM

Reprinted in 2019

© 2015 by The Associated Board of the Royal Schools of Music

AB 3821

Illustrations by Willie Ryan, www.illustrationweb.com/willieryan
Book design and cover by www.adamhaystudio.com
Music and text origination by Julia Bovee
Printed in England by Halstan & Co. Ltd, Amersham, Bucks., on materials from sustainable sources

Dear Singer,

Joining the Dots will help you to sing music from notation and learn new songs more quickly and easily.

In this book you will find lots of ideas to help with the Grade 1 Singing exam and with your sight-singing generally. You will find it best if you work through the book from beginning to end, with your teacher's help.

There are several different things to do:

 Workouts to develop your sense of rhythm and pitch

 Make Music in which you can explore musical ideas

 It Takes Two – music to sing with another singer or a pianist

 **Read and Sing** where there are a number of short songs to sing – read the title to set the mood, work out the rhythm, find the notes and, when you're ready, sing the song right through without stopping!

On the last page of the book you'll find **Songs with Words**, featuring two songs for you to learn.

Enjoy singing, and enjoy Joining the Dots!

Alan Bullard

Contents

Workout 1

Tapping the beat

- Create a steady beat by gently tapping the fingers of one hand, perhaps on the palm of the other hand or on a desk
- There are four crotchet beats in the bar – tap the first beat of each bar slightly louder
- Count '**1**–2–3–4' out loud, but in the first bar only
- Keep in time: don't get faster or slower, or louder and louder!

Rhythm

Here are some rhythms in 4/4 time. In this book, there are always four crotchet beats in the bar.

- Sing these phrases to any suitable syllable while tapping the beat (or pulse)
- Your teacher will play or sing the starting note, or show it to you on the piano
- Sing back the starting note and tap two bars of crotchets before you begin
- Take a breath during the crotchet rest in the middle – but keep tapping the beat!

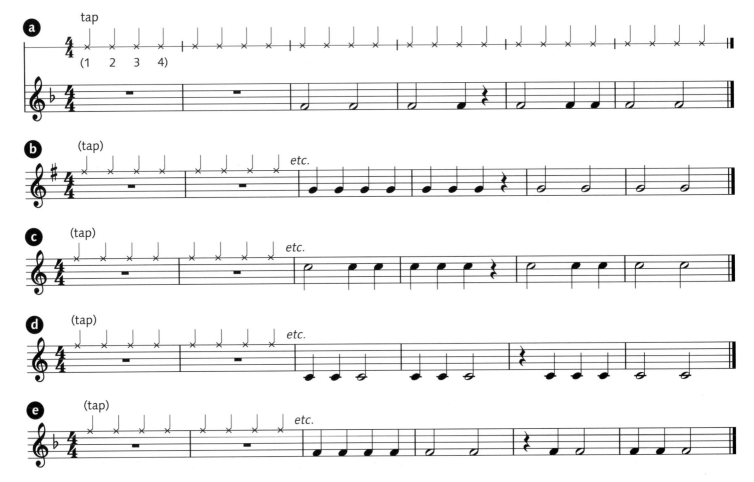

4

Workout 2

F major

1   2   3
doh ray me

Singing back

- Make a tune with your teacher by echoing each phrase in time, without looking at the music
- Your teacher will play you the key-chord and first note, and count in two bars
- You can both tap the beat throughout
- The option is given for singing to numbers or to tonic sol-fa

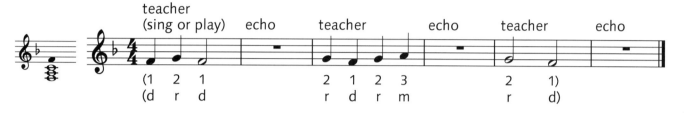

Rhythm and notes

Rhythm and notes, together, are the essential starting point of singing a tune. A great way to sight-sing is to focus on these two elements one by one, and then put them both together.

This tune is in the key of **F major**, and it begins and ends on the note F. Notice that the notes always move 'by step', to the next note up or down – the same is true of all the tunes in this book.

Listen to the key-chord and starting note, and then prepare the tune like this:

- Sing the rhythm on the starting note only, while tapping the beat

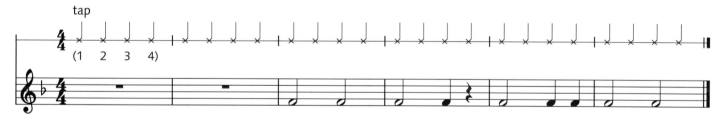

- Then sing all the notes (or pitches) in **free time**: you can sing them to any syllable, or to note names, numbers or tonic sol-fa – just follow the notes up and down as you sing

- Lastly, put rhythm and notes together, tapping the beat quietly throughout

When you have a new tune to sing, always remember: rhythm first, then notes, then both together!

Workout 3

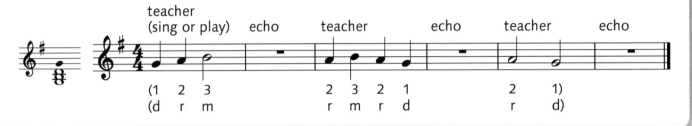

Singing back

- Make a tune with your teacher by echoing each phrase in time, without looking at the music
- Your teacher will play you the key-chord and first note, and count in two bars
- You can both tap the beat throughout

Rhythm and notes

Here are some tunes in the key of **G major**, starting and finishing on the note G. In this book, all the tunes begin and end on the 1st note of the scale (the key-note, or 'doh').

- Listen to the key-chord and starting note
- Sing the rhythm on the starting note only, while tapping the beat
- Then sing all the notes in free time
- Lastly, put rhythm and notes together, tapping the beat quietly throughout

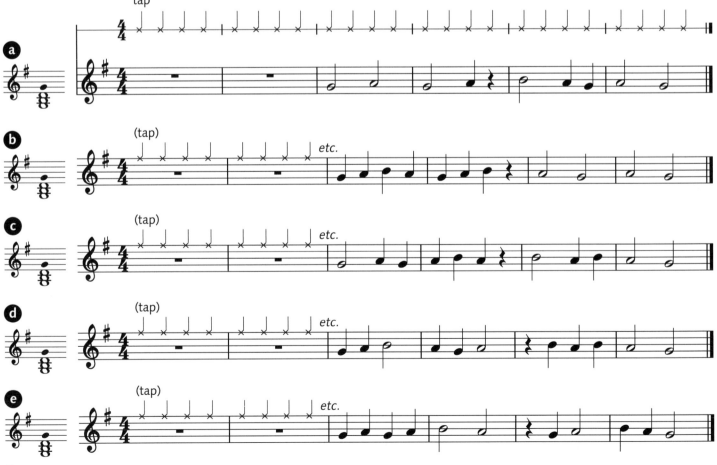

Workout 4

Singing back

- Make a tune with your teacher by echoing each phrase in time, without looking at the music
- Your teacher will play you the key-chord and first note, and count in two bars
- You can both tap the beat throughout

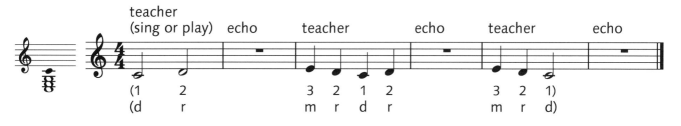

Rhythm and notes

These tunes are in the key of **C major**.

- Listen to the key-chord and starting note
- Sing the rhythm on the starting note only, while tapping the beat
- Then sing all the notes in free time
- Lastly, put rhythm and notes together, tapping the beat quietly throughout

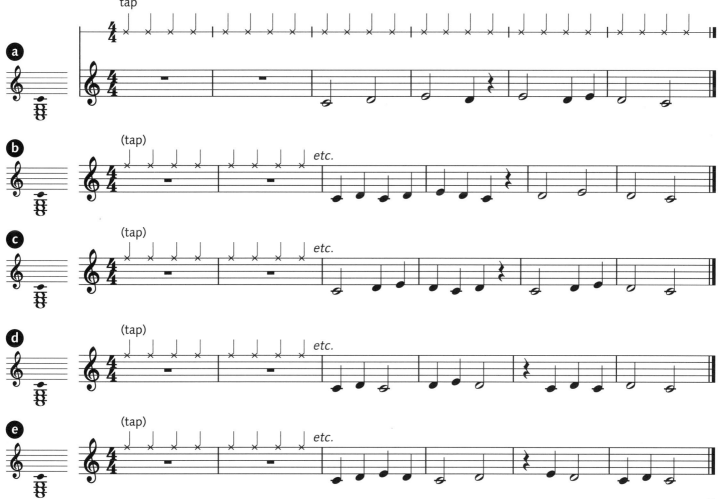

Make Music

My Cat

Make a song to fit the words below:
- First, say the words out loud several times to make a rhythm in 4/4 time
- Play an F on the piano and start your song on that note
- See if you can finish on the note F too!

My black cat's called Daisy; she's very lazy.

A Song in Time

- Play a G on the piano
- Sing this rhythm on the note G several times, to any syllable (tapping the beat if you like)
- Now make the rhythm into a tune, starting and finishing on G

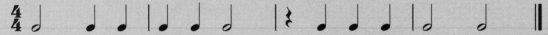

It Takes Two

Here are two duets to sing with your teacher or another pupil, followed by two songs for voice and piano. You can sing these using any suitable syllable.

Patterns in the Sky

- Check the time signature, tempo and key signature, and listen to the key-chord and starting note
- Sing the rhythm on the starting note, counting in two bars before you start (you can do this together)
- On your own, sing the notes in free time and then combine rhythm and notes – then sing the duet together
- Notice that the two voices start and finish together, and that Voice 2 goes higher than Voice 1 in the middle!

Echoing Footsteps

- In this round, you both sing the same music – practise the rhythm first and then the notes
- Voice 2 starts when Voice 1 reaches the ✱ sign
- Repeat several times, if you wish

It Takes Two (continued)

Prepare *On the Move* like this:

- Check the time signature, tempo and key signature, and listen to the key-chord and starting note
- Sing the rhythm on the starting note only, while tapping the beat

- Then sing all the notes in free time – repeat until you are sure that they are right

- Now put rhythm and notes together
- Note that this song is marked *f*, so sing it loudly and cheerfully!
- When you are ready to sing with the piano, listen again to the key-chord and starting note, and tap two bars before you start – keep tapping quietly while you sing
- Always keep going, even if you make a mistake

On the Move

By the Lake

- Take the same step-by-step approach as for *On the Move* (above) – rhythm first, then notes in free time, then both together
- Note that this song is in the key of G major, starting and ending on that note
- It is marked *p*, so sing it quietly and calmly

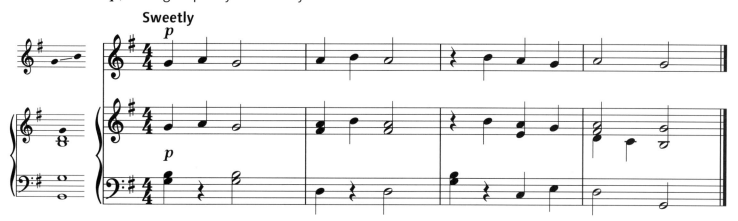

Workout 5

Singing back

- Make a tune with your teacher by echoing each phrase in time, without looking at the music
- Your teacher will play you the key-chord and first note, and count in two bars
- You can both tap the beat throughout

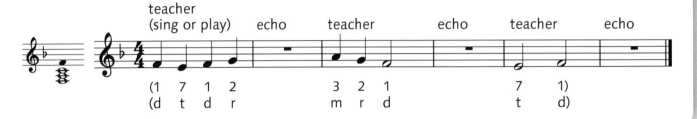

Rhythm and notes

These tunes are in either F major or G major. On this page, and in most of the following Workouts, the tunes now include notes above and below the key-note, while still always beginning and ending on the key-note.

- Check the key signature, and listen to the key-chord and starting note
- Sing the rhythm on the starting note only, while tapping the beat
- Then sing all the notes in free time
- Lastly, put rhythm and notes together, tapping the beat quietly throughout

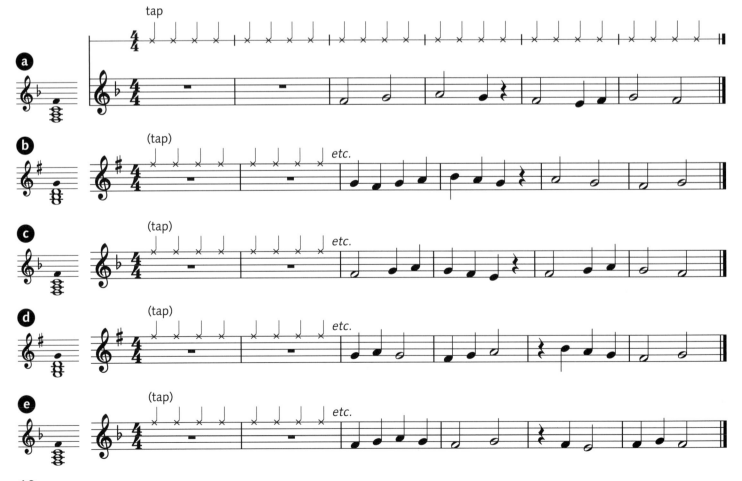

Workout 6

Singing back

- Make a tune with your teacher by echoing each phrase in time, without looking at the music
- Your teacher will play you the key-chord and first note, and count in two bars
- You can both tap the beat throughout

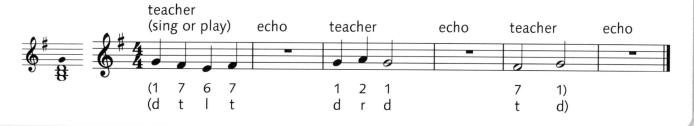

Rhythm and notes

Here are some more tunes in F major and G major.

- Check the key signature, and listen to the key-chord and starting note
- Sing the rhythm on the starting note only, while tapping the beat
- Then sing all the notes in free time
- Lastly, put rhythm and notes together, tapping the beat quietly throughout

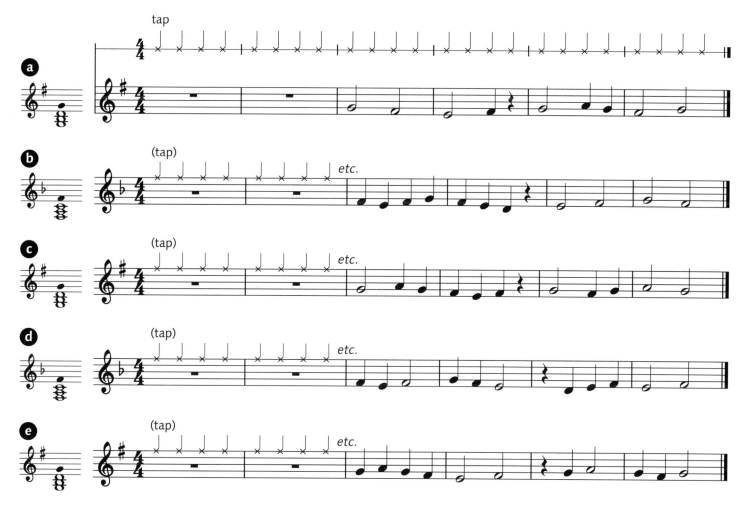

Workout 7

Singing back

- Make a tune with your teacher by echoing each phrase in time, without looking at the music
- Your teacher will play you the key-chord and first note, and count in two bars
- You can both tap the beat throughout

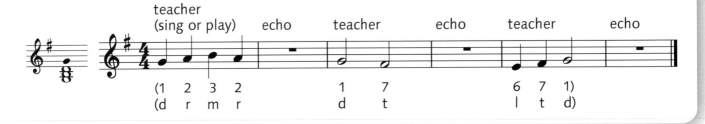

Rhythm and notes

The tunes on this page, and in the following Workouts, now include a slightly wider range.

- Check the key signature, and listen to the key-chord and starting note
- Sing the rhythm on the starting note only, while tapping the beat
- Then sing all the notes in free time
- Lastly, put rhythm and notes together, tapping the beat quietly throughout

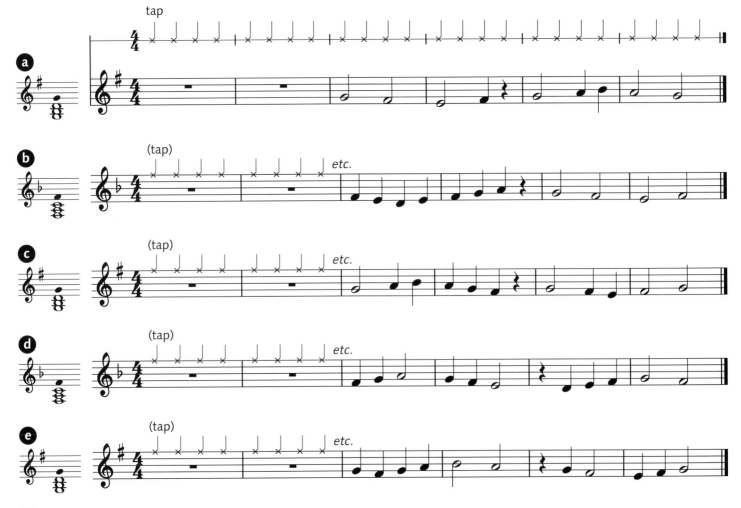

Workout 8

C major
1 2 3 4 5
doh ray me fah soh

F major
1 2 3 4 5
doh ray me fah soh

Singing back

- Make a tune with your teacher by echoing each phrase in time, without looking at the music
- Your teacher will play you the key-chord and first note, and count in two bars
- You can both tap the beat throughout

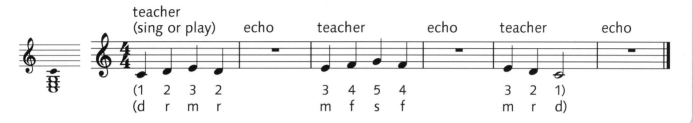

teacher
(sing or play)   echo   teacher   echo   teacher   echo

(1 2 3 2   3 4 5 4   3 2 1)
(d r m r   m f s f   m r d)

Rhythm and notes

These tunes are in C major and F major.

- Check the key signature, and listen to the key-chord and starting note
- Sing the rhythm on the starting note only, while tapping the beat
- Then sing all the notes in free time
- Lastly, put rhythm and notes together, tapping the beat quietly throughout

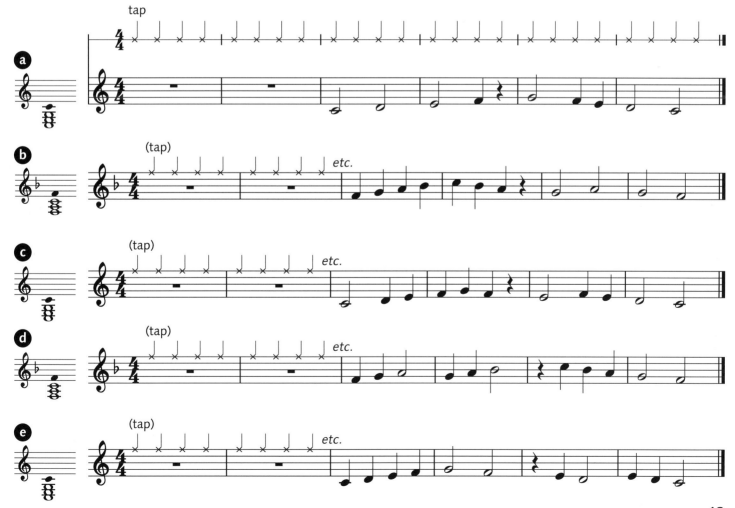

Make Music

Window Shopping

Make a song to fit the words below:
- First, say the words out loud several times to make a rhythm in 4/4 time
- Now make it into a song in the key of G major
- Start and finish on the note G

Walking down the high street, looking in the shops.

Marching By

- Sing this rhythm on the note C several times, to any syllable
- Now make the rhythm into a tune in the key of C major
- Start and finish on the note C

Like a march

It Takes Two

Here are two more duets to sing with your teacher or another pupil, followed by three pages of songs for voice and piano.

A Confident Answer

- Before you sing this duet, prepare it in the same way as for *Patterns in the Sky* on page 8 – rhythm first, then notes in free time, then rhythm and notes combined
- Notice the expression marks – *p* (quiet) and *f* (loud)

Dancing Duet

- In this round, Voice 2 starts when Voice 1 reaches the ✳ sign
- Repeat several times, if you wish

It Takes Two (continued)

Prepare *Sunshine and Clouds* like this:

- Check the time signature, tempo and key signature, and listen to the key-chord and starting note
- Sing the rhythm on the starting note only, while tapping the beat

- Then sing all the notes in free time – repeat until you are sure that they are right

- Now put rhythm and notes together
- Note that the first part of this song is loud and the second part is quiet
- When you are ready to sing with the piano, listen again to the key-chord and starting note, and tap two bars before you start – keep tapping quietly while you sing
- Always keep going, even if you make a mistake

Sunshine and Clouds

Spring Song

- Take the same step-by-step approach as for *Sunshine and Clouds* (above)
- Note that this song begins quietly and ends loudly

It Takes Two (continued)

Always remember:
- Rhythm first, then notes in free time, then both together
- Look out for the *f* and *p* markings

Up and Down

By the River

Starry Night

Nearly Home

Distant Horizon

Over the Bridge

Workout 9

Copy the rhythm

- Echo this rhythm with your teacher by singing back each phrase in time, without looking at the music
- Your teacher will count in two bars before starting
- You can both tap the beat throughout

Rhythm

These rhythms in 4/4 time include pairs of quavers.

- Sing these phrases to any suitable syllable while tapping the beat
- Your teacher will play or sing the starting note, or show it to you on the piano
- Remember to take a breath during the crotchet rest in the middle – but keep tapping the beat!

Workout 10

Singing back

- Make a tune with your teacher by echoing each phrase in time, without looking at the music
- Your teacher will play you the key-chord and first note, and count in two bars
- You can both tap the beat throughout

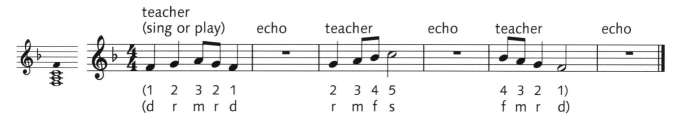

Rhythm and notes

- Check the key signature, and listen to the key-chord and starting note
- Sing the rhythm on the starting note only, while tapping the beat
- Then sing all the notes in free time
- Lastly, put rhythm and notes together, tapping the beat quietly throughout

19

Workout 11

Singing back

- Make a tune with your teacher by echoing each phrase in time, in the same way as before

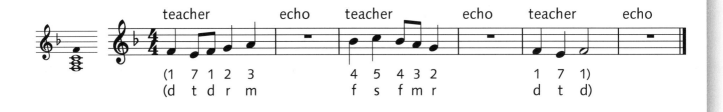

Rhythm and notes

These tunes, and those that follow, have the slightly wider pitch range of a 6th.

- Sing the rhythm on the starting note first, followed by all the notes in free time – then put rhythm and notes together

20

Workout 12

Singing back

- Make a tune with your teacher by echoing each phrase in time

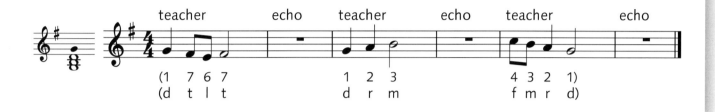

Rhythm and notes

- Sing the rhythm on the starting note first, followed by all the notes in free time – then put rhythm and notes together

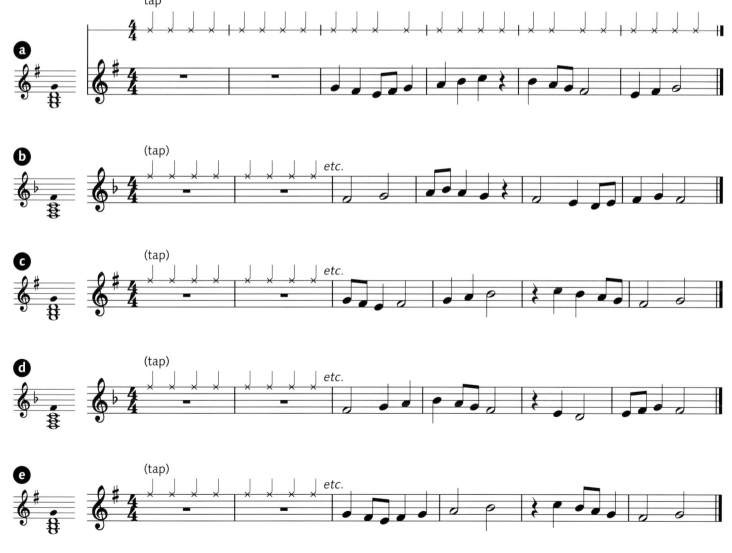

Workout 13

Singing back

- Make a tune with your teacher by echoing each phrase in time

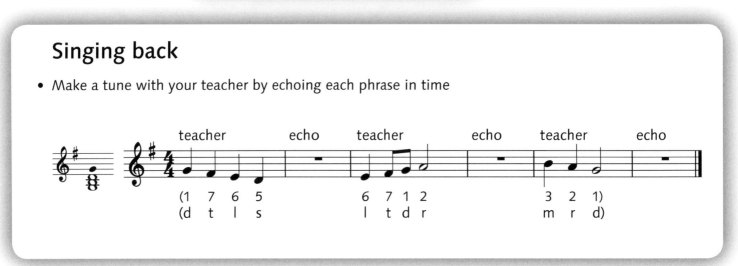

Rhythm and notes

- Remember – rhythm first, then notes, then both together!

22

Workout 14

Singing back

• Make a tune with your teacher by echoing each phrase in time

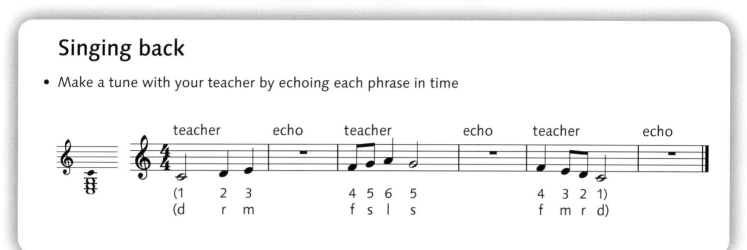

Rhythm and notes

• Remember – rhythm first, then notes, then both together!

Make Music

Cycle Champion

Make a song to fit the words below:
- First, say the words out loud several times to make a rhythm in 4/4 time
- Now make it into a song in the key of G major
- Start and finish on the note G

Up in the front is Speedy Jack, racing along the cycle track.

The Day Begins

- Sing this rhythm on the note F several times, to any syllable
- Now make the rhythm into a tune in the key of F major
- Start and finish on the note F

Lively

It Takes Two

Here are two more duets to sing with your teacher or another pupil, followed by two songs for voice and piano.

Summer Time

Remember:
- Rhythm first, then notes in free time, then rhythm and notes combined – then sing the duet together

Stepping Out

- In this round, Voice 2 starts when Voice 1 reaches the ✱ sign
- Repeat several times, if you wish

It Takes Two (continued)

Prepare *Late Again!* like this:

- Check the time signature, tempo and key signature, and listen to the key-chord and starting note
- Sing the rhythm on the starting note only, while tapping the beat

- Then sing all the notes in free time – repeat until you are sure that they are right

- Now put rhythm and notes together
- Note that this song begins loudly, then gets quiet, then loud again
- When you are ready to sing with the piano, listen again to the key-chord and starting note, and tap two bars before you start – keep tapping quietly while you sing
- Always keep going, even if you make a mistake

Late Again!

Evening Calm

- In this song there is a crescendo hairpin and a diminuendo hairpin – move from quiet to louder, and back again, as smoothly as you can!

Read and Sing

Here are some more songs to practise sight-singing with piano, similar to the tests in the ABRSM Grade 1 Singing exam.

- Make sure you can sing the rhythm while tapping the beat
- Then sing the notes in free time
- Now put rhythm and notes together, tapping two bars quietly before you begin
- Always remember to keep going in time with the piano, even if you make a mistake

Walk On

Daydreamer

Blue Sky

Read and Sing (continued)

Cat and Mouse

Hill-Climbing

Peaceful Thoughts

Read and Sing (continued)

The End of the Day

Shining Bright

Folk Dance

Read and Sing (continued)

Smooth and Solemn

Aiming High

Looking Down the Well

Read and Sing (continued)

Celebration

Approaching the Shore

Time for Tea

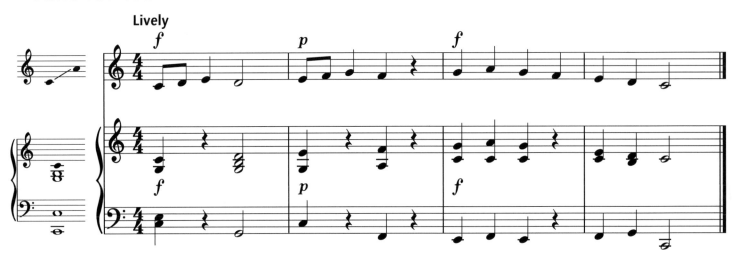

Read and Sing (continued)

For those who wish to practise reading both clefs, here are some songs from pages 27–8, now in the bass clef.

The End of the Day

Cat and Mouse

Folk Dance

Songs with Words

Here are two songs that you can learn to sing. The first can be sung by a group of singers, divided into up to five parts; the second can be sung solo or by a group of singers, with piano.

Crotchets and Quavers

- Learn this round by singing it all together first
- Then split into parts – any number from two to five
- Each new part comes in when the previous part reaches the * sign
- Sing it through as many times as you like!

Stead - y crot - chet, qua - ver af - ter qua - ver in a row, And qua - ver, qua - ver crot - chet back we go!

Running Up and Down Again

- Here's a song to help with moving up and down the scale!

Run-ning up and down a-gain to E D C. (me ray doh.) Run-ning up and down a-gain to F E D. (fah me ray.)

Run-ning up and down a-gain to C D E F G A G F E D C. (doh ray me fah soh lah soh fah me ray doh.)